C
b
for

Shops and Shopping

Newcastle City Libraries

**Published by Newcastle City Libraries
© Newcastle upon Tyne City Libraries, 1986.**

ISBN 0-902653-47-4

Introduction

In this volume of our 'Gone but not Forgotten' series, we try to cover as many aspects as possible of Newcastle as a shopping centre, from the humble street trader to the largest department stores.

These photographs illustrate the contrast between shopping facilities today and those of earlier generations. Most marked is the change from small specialised shops, often dealing in only one commodity, to the large multiple retailers and department stores of today.

Another contrast is disappearance of the 'personal service' aspect of shopping. This is best seen here in the interior view of Lowe and Moorhouse, drapers, with its chairs for customers and attentive staff.

One aspect of shopping in earlier times which is emphasised quite strongly in the selection of photographs is the great contrast of social class - the great gulf between rich and poor. Compare the elegant ladies at the Fenwick sale with those searching for serviceable old clothes at "Paddy's Market".

Towards the end of the nineteenth century Newcastle developed as a regional shopping centre, attracting custom from all over the north east and beyond. At the same time Northumberland Street became the main shopping area which it remains today.

1. This view of Humble's basket shop in the Cloth Market has no real right to be in this selection as the buildings were demolished long before living memory, but it earns its place as one of the most fascinating pictures of old Newcastle. Photographed in 1858.

2. 'Shoe-lace Tommy': one of Newcastle's many Victorian street traders, about 1880.

3. An affectionately remembered rendezvous: Tilley's Cafe and Restaurant in Blackett Street, around the turn of the century.

4. The old clothes market in Sandgate, about 1890. In the right background, one of the City's many alehouses.

5. Fowl, dead and alive! 1890.

6. Crowds throng Fenwick's, Northumberland Street, for the great summer sale of 1898.

7. Tyler's Boot Palace, average price 14/6d (72½p) in 1900. This firm owned five shops in the City; this is probably in either Grainger Street or Clayton Street.

8. Mrs Richardson, fruit-seller, photographed at her pitch outside the Central
Station, 1900.

9. 'Umbrellas covered in half an hour' at J.G. Scott's shop,
   Pilgrim Street about 1900.

10. "Paddy's Market", Quayside, 1900.

11. 'Look here, 200 young rabbits,' some on
display, at the Northern Counties Meat
Company's shop, Shields Road, about
1907.

OLD
PORT
WINES
A FINE OLD VINTAGE

30/ 36/ 42/
2/6 3/ 36

CALLEYVAT
WHISKY
IS
FAMOUS
FOR
ITS
HIGH
CLASS
QUALITY.

12. The Victoria Wine Company's shop in Blackett Street,
1908.

13. Part of the Green Market and Newgate Street, about 1910.

14. Bainbridge's, the city's oldest established department store, founded in 1838. Photographed about 1910.

15. The interior of Stewardson's, chemists, 17 Elswick Road,
about 1910.

16. The Quayside Sunday market is still going strong; here it is in about 1915.

17. A typical general dealer's shop. Broad-
chare, 1921.

18. These little shops on Percy Street, at the corner of Leazes Park Road, are remembered with affection. They were demolished in the mid-1960's.

19. Department store shopping in a more leisurely age at Lowe and Moorhouse, corner of Blackett and Northumberland Streets, 1932.

20. A moose's head serves as a hat-stand at a bookstall in the Bigg Market. 1938.

21. Toy-seller outside Boots', Grainger Street, December
1939.